ROPE
ROPE

by the same author

poetry
A WORD FROM THE LOKI
FLOODS
CONFIDENTIAL REPORTS
(translations of Maltese poet Immanuel Mifsud)
THE MOON HAS WRITTEN YOU A POEM
(adapted from the Portuguese of José Jorge Letria)
THE HOLY LAND
THE WATER STEALER
THE PLAY OF WAVES
(translations of Maltese poet Immanuel Mifsud)
SHOULDER TAP
SELECTED POEMS

editor
A QUARK FOR MISTER MARK:
101 Poems about Science
(with Jon Turney)
WILD RECKONING:
An Anthology Provoked by Rachel Carson's Silent Spring
(with John Burnside)
HART CRANE:
Selected Poems
DARK MATTER:
Poems of Space
(with Jocelyn Bell Burnell)
THE FINEST MUSIC:
Early Irish Lyrics

MAURICE RIORDAN

ROPE

faber

First published in 2026
by Faber & Faber Ltd
The Bindery, 51 Hatton Garden
London EC1N 8HN

Typeset by Faber & Faber Ltd
Printed and bound by CPI Group (UK) Ltd, Croydon CR0 4YY

A CIP record for this book
is available from the British Library

ISBN 978-0-571-40148-2

Printed and bound in the UK on FSC® certified paper in line with our continuing
commitment to ethical business practices, sustainability and the environment.
For further information see faber.co.uk/environmental-policy

Our authorised representative in the EU for product safety is
Easy Access System Europe, Mustamäe tee 50, 10621 Tallinn, Estonia
gpsr.requests@easproject.com

2 4 6 8 10 9 7 5 3 1

for Kathryn

1

'The eternity of things in itself or in God' – Pascal – 'must also astonish our brief duration.'

This morning my optician, Angelo, described himself as the Luckiest Man Alive. I enquired in what way. He told me he jumped out of bed first thing thinking *this will be the happiest day of my life*. What had occurred yesterday, and the days before, was of no consequence and could never cloud the lovely prospect of the morning. It's a philosophy. As serviceable as any. But it is the opposite of Montaigne's, who found consolation in the past and the accumulations of memory. I'm with Angelo by aspiration; in temperament I confess I follow Montaigne.

You must always engage in conversation, whenever possible, with your eye doctors. They are looking into what once were the windows to the soul. Our eyes are no longer that. But they are the most brilliant, active, expressive and colourful of the features – an organ, moreover, not specially human but one we share with countless life forms. The eye has arisen separately in many species, both extant and extinct, as though the blind energy of carbon chemistry yearns for the light and, from the ammonite to the owl, it has fuelled the evolutionary quest of sight. Eyesight is the faculty that gives us most readily the sensation of aliveness in the arena of creation. In a literal sense, it achieves a victory of light over darkness. Opticians and ophthalmologists spend hours behind instruments in windowless rooms peering closely at the eye's intricate interface with the brain. Something of the mystery may have filtered through to them.

this other yoke

Do I have a soul? Wrong question. Does my body have a soul? Better – since there is an entity in me, or part of me, that experiences time differently to the body. 'My' body – wonderful creature it is – has grown, matured, declined and will soon decay. Whereas this other yoke (my soul, let's say), although it too changes, does not change in accordance with an inexorable temporal process. It appears to have strengthened and clarified since my twenties and seems to acquire both generous and more ignoble impulses as I get old. But those developments are reversible and are separate from my body's. Alas, it (the other yoke) isn't, I suspect, separable from the body. Homer's Trojan warriors bled out the *psyche* – their souls – on the sand. That was it.

the scales

My religious upbringing left me a few things. One is the need that my life be judged. Weighed up. My many sins of commission and omission put in one pan; my worthy, kind, forgiving, selfless thoughts and deeds stacked in the other. My fear is that as one pan is heaped high with evidence of a dutiful and fairly decent life, one act of omission, or else some secret failure of love, will outweigh it.

I grew up on a farm. 'The poet's equivalent' – Les Murray – 'of being born with a silver spoon in your mouth.' Touché. The most surprising fact about this farm was it had (where exactly, no one knew) un-marked Famine graves. That people could have starved on such land was beyond imagining: rolling pasture laden with the fruits of the earth, and a few miles to the south – along the Atlantic coast from Roche's Point to Youghal – fruits of the sea. As a child, I fantasised of running away and living in the wild quite feasibly throughout the seasons of the year.

And yet: 'Out of every corner of the wood and glens they came creeping forth upon their hands, for their legs could not bear them; they looked Anatomies [of] death, they spoke like ghosts, crying out of their graves; they did eat of the carrions, happy where they could find them, yea, and one another soon after, in so much as the very carcasses they spared not to scrape out of their graves; and if they found a plot of water-cresses or shamrocks, there they flocked as to a feast for the time, yet not able long to continue therewithal; that in a short space there were none almost left, and a most populous and plentiful country suddenly left void of man or beast.' Edmund Spenser, writing in the 1580s about the aftermath of the Geraldine wars. Munster was a place of mass death across centuries, but this was not caused by natural disaster, potato blight, disease or straightforward killing.

*Caliban &
Prospero*

I marvelled – still do – how Spenser (a *colon*) wrote so well of my native places, that he could configure the topography, from the little rivers around Kilcolman to Galteemore on the skyline, with such delight and intimacy, knowing the place lore, even a few words of the language. Yet he advocated the extermination of the people and was an official observer at the massacre of Smerwick. Ireland was his Caliban, the 'born devil on whose nature / Nurture can never stick'. And he was Prospero, a man of books and imagination. It was an Isle, even so, more than worthy of his powers.

In Munster in the 1580s and the decades following, the same ideology that worked to colonise North America, and elsewhere, got its trial run.

Caliban = the Giant (I forget his name, if he had one) in Book V of *The Faerie Queene*, who is hurled back into the sea. He represents for me something not far off Marxism.

Spenser, I'd be with those who burned you out of Kilcolman; Caliban, I'll bring treats to in his prison cave.

Summers a teenager I drove East Cork gathering pea samples from pea-fields. I revved the van down boreens through tunnels of hawthorn and honeysuckle into whitewashed farmyards. Neverending weeks, I was lost among dairy herds and barley; parked beside rook-haunted Norman ruins; sat it out under the soft copious rain; hopped over a rotting stile into a paddock of inquisitive purebreds; followed lime-covered avenues that unwound onto manor houses next the Bride or Blackwater. Skylarks in morning drizzle, herons, corn bunting, stotting hares. I masturbated beside a pond curtained with sunlight, ate my cheese-and-bacon on a couch of bracken in a ring fort, had a shit inside a cathedral of ancient beech. *J'ai embrassé l'aube d'été!* I drove at speed down a dirt-track and swivelled to a stop above the ocean.

John Montague, as I showed him round my childhood places, surprised me saying the muse of this part of the island is a handsome young earl. Not one of your fertility deities then, the goddesses he found in Robert Graves and the Clogher Valley of *Tír Eoghain*, but a young O'Brien, or a Fitzgerald or Barry from the old Norman-Irish stock, was tutelary of this land of Eden, as fat as Normandy and Somerset. We were driving among wheatfields, orchards, polytunnels, herds of Friesians and, courteously waving us on, carrot-headed youngsters aboard tractors and combines.

l'aube d'été

a sleeping earl

The relationship between a writer's life and their work (at least between poet and poem) is *umbilical* – that's to say, the poem is nourished by the bloodstream of the poet, but the whole fearful, ecstatic effort of invention and composition is to give the poem independent life.

fictional tangents

One requirement: a fictional tangent that gives the stuff impetus, sends it away just a little at first, but then utterly and forever, from the writer and the ecstasy and misfortune of their life.

fictional space

Zadie Smith's story 'The Embassy of Cambodia' has the embassy surrounded by a high brick wall. Behind it, a game of badminton is always in progress. The racquets can be heard from the street and the shuttlecock seen flying back and forth overhead. But the players are hidden from sight. I drive by the Cambodian Embassy in north-west London. There's a brick wall all right, but it's only waist high. That raised wall sealed off the embassy and created the story's fictional space – just as when Dante, astray in an Italian wood, meets the leopard.

Borges & Dante

Borges described the *Inferno* as God's justice visited on a small district of medieval Italy, as administered by one man.

Borges said Dante wrote his great poem so he could imagine meeting Beatrice again (and imagine her spurning him again). I'd say Borges knew whereof he spoke. His story 'The Aleph' is – among other things – at once an avowal of unrequited love, for the narrator's departed Beatriz, and an act of exquisite literary revenge. 'Borges' denies his vision of the mystical Aleph in the cellar, i.e. the underworld, in order to crush his rival, the bad poet Daneri, who is Beatriz's first cousin. The narrator then relates how Daneri achieves literary renown while he, 'Borges', remains in provincial obscurity. Of course we're reading Borges; the rival's work is forgotten, his real-life name unknown.

In Borges's imagination, Daneri and Beatriz were lovers. The narrator 'Borges' sees them in the Aleph, abandoned and shameless, how could he not – but he doesn't say so, only notes the secret drawer containing obscene 'precise' letters Beatriz had written her cousin.

One almost forgets it was Dante put Francesca and Paolo (his childhood friend) in Hell, along with all the others. Why? Spite. Borges: '[they] were obscure emblems of the joy he did not attain . . . forever united in their *Inferno*'.

Keats took Cary's 1814 Dante – in a lightweight pocket-size edition – on his six-week walking tour with Brown in the summer of 1818 to the Lakes and Scotland. One night the following April he dreamt of Paolo and Francesca – or rather he dreamt *he* was in

Hell and 'floated about . . . with a beautiful figure to whose lips mine were joined'. He and Fanny Brawne were the damned lovers. Or were they perhaps Dante and Beatrice? When he sailed for Rome, he left the Dante with Fanny. She was a stylish, fashion-savvy young woman whose fate it was to be muse of a sickly, impecunious genius. She wrote out 'Bright Star' in a brisk cursive on the flyleaf of her Dante.

The most detailed, and grossly disproportionate, feature in late medieval maps of Ireland is Lough Derg – a nondescript, drear little lake in Donegal with an island that was, and remains, a place of pilgrimage, it being after all a rare entrance to Hell.

literary
ambition

folly of

When I indulge, as I do, the folly of literary ambition – that perhaps a handful of my poems will be read years after I die – I know this can bring no satisfaction, since I will not be around any more. Or if the religion of my childhood prove me wrong, I'll exist in a state where fame will not be a category of that existence. I am grateful even so, immoderately and irrationally grateful, for all those writers of the past who displayed this same foolishness.

My life has been enriched almost as much by the Psalms and the *Iliad* as by iPhones and internal combustion engines.

My boast as a writer would be never to have written
a bad sentence. That I may have written many half-
truths or dishonest things doesn't seem to come into it.

This could be my favourite sentence. 'He was (indeed)
honest, and of an open, and free nature: had an ex-
cellent fancy; brave notions, and gentle expressions:
wherein he flowed with that facility, that sometime
it was necessary he should be stopped.' Ben Jonson
on Shakespeare.

One can't but hear English prose fall away after Jon-
son. It withdrew in exhaustion from the arm-wrestle
between (classical) Latin syntax and a recalcitrant
Germanic word-hoard. It became linear and pliant,
softer, fluent, easier. Boy, am I glad!

I love the ball-bearings of English, the little words,
all those conjunctive prepositions of time and place
that lubricate the sentence, the paragraph, the poem.
Slippery, and full of mischief, they also drive me nuts.

'Come on out right now from in under that table!'
Could you reprimand your grandchild just so in an-
other language?

Or start a great poem as Robert Frost does? 'Back out
of all this now too much for us'.

'When you add a comma or add or subtract a word, and the thing reacts and changes' – Deborah Eisenberg – 'it's so exciting that you forget how absolutely terrible writing feels a lot of the time.' Poetry is the one place where this obsession with style can be (almost) satisfied.

style By style I mean such qualities as decorum, tone, syntax, tension, rapidity – and the overall harmony of elements that constitutes formal completeness.

tone By tone I mean a quality – beyond that of voice – that's analogous to 'muscle tone'.

voice The false voice of a poem will surely come first. Several false voices there may be, each pitched too high and wanting to impress. The real voice, if it comes, has something of a growl.

The lines of the poem appear, disappear, reappear as it advances – as if a dream is remembering itself. It's a magical script that ideally would be writ on water. That would then instantly freeze.

There is a moment when the scraps of thought and random images one has on screen, or in one's head, suddenly seem to shift into patterns, as when a magnet is passed under iron filings on a paper sheet, and there's the outline of some immanent overall pattern.

I say 'suddenly', but it can be more a dawning, or a recognisable shape emerging as on an old-fashioned photographic film. Once glimpsed, the completion of the poem then feels inevitable – it becomes dynamic and often, in fact, easy.

I'd distinguish between the *gross motor* of a poem and its *fine motor*. The first is what makes the poem strong, active, obvious – just as the body's big muscles enable one to stand and walk across a stage. The poem's fine motor involves all the delicate fingering and gesturing – those (almost innumerable) details of register, syntax, tense, lineation, metrics.

Big Muscle

Form is Big Muscle. It's that aura of fitness. Everything toned.

By form I don't just mean villanelle, sestina, pantoum, and so on. All good, all potentially heavy lifting. But nothing's more formally perfect, and powerful, than Psalm 139, 'Out of the Cradle Endlessly Rocking', 'The Swimmer'. It's the robust effect of proportion and steady exertion.

When browsing the poetry shelves of, for example, Foyles, I have – many times – bought a book on the strength of two or three poems that caught my eye skimming through. Then when home I've read the book at leisure, I see oh that was it: just those few are good, maybe a couple more. This isn't to do with my uncanny literary discernment! But with how, obscurely, the brain reads. We scan the page down as well as across, unconsciously picking up cues. We see patterns – and somehow the overall pattern – very quickly. There is an old psychologist's test where you're shown up close a page consisting of rectangles in shades of grey and black. Then you look at the same page from, say, ten paces off – and the pattern resolves into the face of Abraham Lincoln. That's how the brain first recognises a poem.

Alas, there are readers, critics, editors and indeed many practitioners who suffer from the equivalent of prosopagnosia.

'[The] light escape' – Emily Dickinson – 'Into the Beautiful' is the wish of every poem.

Poems in the late nineteenth century spent so many evenings in drawing rooms they became sweet, conventional and insipid. By my lifetime – in the last century – poems had spent so many hours in seminar rooms they became clever, tortuous and anaemic. Latterly, in this century, poems have become something else again: sincere, victimy, tuneless – and hypocritical, as they turned into a transient currency of social capital.

To say a poem is, as one reads these days in reviews, 'sincere' is equivalent to praising Rogier van der Weyden's *Portrait of a Lady* as 'a true likeness' – the sitter being long dead, and of whom no other likeness exists.

'All that is only for the sake of the author' – Pascal – 'is worthless.'

AI (artificial intelligence) will soon be proficient at writing poems. It's a formulaic activity. Two good-sounding lines and *voilà*, you generate a formally impressive villanelle. Ditto, or similarly, pantoum and triolet. (We won't speak of the sestina!) The ballad requires too much invention, the haiku's for dabblers, but lists, anaphora and sonnets still have air in the tyres.

AI poetry

Among the traditional forms, the sonnet is your roller case: simple, useful, a marvel of design, but strictly compact and needing careful packing. It almost seems – perhaps is – infinitely variable in what it will hold. No mystery about it though. The ratio of octet to sestet 4:3 is about the most obvious non-symmetrical ratio you could hit on. Whereas the Golden Mean, which governs sunflower and seashore, is mysteriously 8:5.

your roller case

It's moot whether there'll be a detectable difference between the AI poem and a human one – I mean other than syntactical muddle and haphazard punctuation (in the carbon-based example).

Any self-respecting AI entity would be *embarrassed* by most published poems these days. In fact, aesthetic embarrassment could become the test for sentience. 'Hey AI(va), aren't you embarrassed by that maudlin poem about cyborg-fluidity in this week's *NYRB*?' Overwhelming stench of burning silicon.

It does look like we've reached the heat death of poetry.

People are stupid. They're taken in by good luck and good looks; are fooled by flattery; serially conned by politicians, prospective romantic partners and by their own journals and social media posts. They follow a trend and listen to crap music or read laborious fiction. They grieve over royals and celebs, entrust their physical and mental wellbeing to charlatans, swallow pills, eat food prepared by disgruntled strangers, buy lottery tickets. They'll spend hours on a crossword or honing a vindictive email. Men will sulk for days after their football team loses. Parents drive at high speed on motorways with their kids in the back.

People are not stupid. Children learn languages, long division, table etiquette. We can master bridge, knitting, plastering, cryptology. We become adept with keyboards and cars; we sing and dance even when we can't play the piano; we laugh at *Father Ted* and enjoy a live concert – prefer, say, Adele to Taylor

Swift – even if we can't read. Humans survive by memory and ingenuity in baked and polar regions; they thrive alike in the labyrinths of the Amazon and the Himalayas. Even so, civilisation privileges a fine edge that enables only a few to play from a musical score, or write an essay.

There's the old chestnut about the monkey with the typewriter who, given world enough and time, would write the complete works of Shakespeare. Though the analogy is defective, it does point to the scale of what's happened: from the genetic lineage of a few hominids a few tens of thousands of generations ago comes all human creativity. Once primitive life got going, it was only a matter of time to the Book of Job, calculus, Château Pétrus, driverless cars . . . and there's no end in sight. That's evolution for you – unless you can put your finger on some divine intervention along the way?

who wrote Shakespeare?

'We wish to suggest a structure for the salt of deoxyribose nucleic acid (D.N.A.). This structure has novel features which are of considerable biological interest.' That's how Crick and Watson begin their paper in *Nature* (25 April 1953). I don't know if there's a classical term for this rhetorical device, but I'll call it the Penny Bluff: the modest bet a writer might proffer to hide a once-in-a-lifetime winning hand.

Penny Bluff

The best example in a poem I can think of is Elizabeth Bishop's opening to 'Santarém': 'Of course I may be re-membering it all wrong'. Of course, she remembers it all so well: the 'under-lit clouds', the blue zebus, rivers full of 'crazy shipping', nuns gaily embarking in white habits, a cow off 'somewhere, to be married'. And then the empty wasps' nest she admires so much in the pharmacy the pharmacist gives it her for free but which, back on board ship, her travelling companion Mr Swan, 'the retiring head of Philips Electric', finds 'ugly'.

There's a moment as EB reads 'Filling Station' when, at the lines 'Somebody waters the plant, / or oils it, may-be', she emits an inebriated chortle at her joke – but also because it is a dirty joke? Oil lubricates and dirt-ies, and that oil-permeated gas station is four times 'dirty'. The oil even gets into – already is *in* – the one item in this dirty world that gives it feminine grace: the hand-embroidered d*oily*.

One feels EB's doily is kin to the dried-out 'exquisite' wasps' nest Mr Swan ('really a very nice old man') tells her is ugly. In a letter to Robert Lowell, EB famously wrote, 'you must say I was the loneliest person who ever lived.'

A Mr Swan, 'who wanted to see the Amazon before he died', did run Philips Electric in the 1950s. One can only wonder what else he saw on the Amazon.

16

'UR 2 GOOD 2 B 4 GOT 10' – Lowell to Bishop (outside of an envelope).

At the end of the paper announcing the exquisite double-helical structure of the DNA molecule, the author (Crick at this point) overplays the under-statement: 'It has not escaped our notice that the specific pairing that we have postulated immediately suggests a possible copying mechanism for the genetic material.' *Crick & Watson*

Erwin Schrödinger: 'how can the events in space and time which take place within the spatial boundary of a living organism be accounted for by physics and chemistry?' In other words, here we are – ruminating on poems and being in love – in a world we only partly understand but understand well enough to know its fabric is formed and governed by universal laws that admit no inconsistency or exception. How to make an entropy-defying triple-jump from chemistry to poems! How come there is, in the inexorable down-hill drain of matter towards heat death, this messy U-bend in which all of life happens? *What Is Life?*

U-bend

The required step Schrödinger had figured (in 1943, before the discovery of the structure of DNA) was a hereditary mechanism. Once you've got the hereditary mechanism you're off on a bender. All you need – and there's no shortage of it! – is time. But how do you *bender*

17

make that first impossible jump to get from entropy-governed physics and chemistry to something as fiendishly complicated as a replicating cell?

The thing about the hereditary mechanism – once it exists – is fallibility, its room for error. This permits mutation, variation, possible adaptation, selection; while random DNA fluctuations (more salient among small populations like early humans) give rise to the capricious outcomes of genetic drift. So over time – over those vast reaches of time we cannot imagine – the labyrinthine structures and spectacular variousness of life emerge. All the ways of error and glory!

Assume there's no mystery, that life is an inevitable, or even possible, product or by-product of physical law. It happens, if not commonly then under conditions that, because of the amount of time and space available, occur again and again – though, given those same scales, we are unlikely ever to encounter advanced life outside this planet. So here we live – or at least have lived thus far – with a conviction of the uniqueness of human destiny, in a universe where evolved life is a naturally occurring phenomenon. And commonplace.

Assume there is a mystery, that the physical universe (plural, if you like) is the instrument of a transcendent being whose plan for humans is much as Judeo-Christian tradition has accorded us. We are a Chosen People. But surely then we are one of many? God would hardly have set up such a splendid gallery for just one infinitesimal – if admittedly rather splendid! – temporary speck.

'It's hard to draw conclusions about if we're common or not, if our specific configuration is everywhere or nowhere' – NASA scientist Jessie Christiansen, who's thinking only of 'our' solar system.

The spuds growing in one field will never have any inkling of the turnips in the next.

Let's say life just got going on the off-chance, without flouting any laws, but is unrelated to other phenomena, in this universe or its kindred, and remains entirely contingent – at least while we stay prisoned within the laws. The great extinctions, the meteorite hits, the ice ages and global deluges: no bother. The gig is under way, endlessly resourceful and inventive, and can only end time after time in the gobsmacking, Attenborough-awesome, multifarious, biological world we struggle to wonder at.

And then, out of nowhere, along come the lad and lass with opposable thumbs, and the monstrous brain.

Let's say, life being entirely contingent, it evolves into the world of the Buddha, Jesus, Muhammad, Francis of Assisi, Harriet Tubman, Black Elk, Mother Teresa. Is not human life, with its moral energy, something other to all else – the spacious universe a mere theatre, albeit a necessary and a marvellous one – and all other life, which is deterministic, lacking volition and blind to its destiny? Obviously so! Say the Platonists, the Church Fathers, the venture capitalists, along with the post-Heideggerian theologians.

Atman &
BrahmanAnd Schrödinger: 'The only possible alternative [to Western belief-systems] is simply to keep to the immediate experience that consciousness is a singular of which the plural is unknown; that there is only one thing and that what seems to be a plurality is merely a series of different aspects of this one thing'. He has tuned to the Upanishads, that oracular station east of Hilversum on the old wireless sets. Which seems the best place to let the matter rest for now.

'Nothing conclusive has yet taken place in the world' – Bakhtin – 'the ultimate word of the world and about the world has not yet been spoken'.

We don't even belong?

For a time in the 1990s Kleenex toilet paper was patterned with Penrose tiles, that is, the aperiodic tiling

20

the eponymous mathematician devised whereby a surface could be tiled forever without once repeating the pattern. It was the solution to an age-old problem. I bought several rolls. But then the line was discontinued, the result as I remember of a lawsuit. A pity – it was ontologically somewhat salutary to wipe my bum while meditating on the tiling of infinity.

My first adventure with satnav was in the company of Jocelyn Bell Burnell. We were driving at night west of Hay-on-Wye in her brand-new Yaris. There was something uncanny about navigating that shape-shifting borderland while being invisibly guided by satellites. And it spoke to the vast, unlikely order of the universe that, in these unlikely circumstances, I was being driven by the first human to have 'heard' pulsars.

The silence between those infinite spaces – it sort of comforts *me*.

You travel out of London, or Los Angeles, say, and let's go by bus, then on foot, so you come after a day or so to a leafy suburb that goes on and on, and you turn into a close or a dead-end street, mid-morning, so quiet, a few cars on the sidewalk, sprinklered lawns, fragrant wistaria-clad houses. Here we are in the suburbs of the universe – inconceivably far from the physical commotion, all that excitement of the atom, remote from the foaming clusters, super-heated gases, colliding galaxies, with their annihilating forces of radiation and gravity. Just a regular weekday morning, laundry spinning, kids at school, time for coffee. 'Siri, put some Dolly Parton on.'

I leave cupboard doors open. Sometimes I bang my head and swear, or someone else bangs their head and swears at me. Is this the wish to hurt myself, or others? It seems not: once, in a previous home, I had a carpenter refit, at some expense, the kitchen cabinets above head height. I think it may have to do with a wish to be myself open, frank, spontaneous – whereas my gift for language, if any, is to hedge even as I speak (that is usually, write) with an open heart and mind.

When my children were small, I developed a habit of keeping paper napkins in my pockets for emergencies – to the extent I'd collect clean (and not so clean) napkins off the dinner table and opportunistically walk off with those I found at parties. My children have reached middle age and no longer need their noses wiped. But recently, after a night out, next day I found several napkins stuffed into my trousers.

I resolved to break my habit with the cupboards. It seemed I'd succeeded. Not one cracked skull in weeks! We invited friends over and I cooked for them. We had an intimate, well-lubricated evening over seafood, cheese and fruit desserts. When they left in the wee hours, I stepped back into the kitchen. Every cupboard door was open.

Freud (like Darwin) could think radically about life – in his case, human consciousness – because he ignored, or suppressed the potential for, any supernatural agency in its origins and being.

The vocation of every doctor since Asclepius has been to free our lives of pain and misery as far as possible. Mostly misguided: the excruciating surgeries, lobotomies, bloodlettings; the chronic unintended transmission of infection; centuries of ignorant certainties about blood-flow, pregnancy, the function of organs and their effect on mental states. Freud, and all that followed, opened up the mind to doctoring – and nowadays holds out the hope *each* individual life has meaning, that anxiety, despair, addiction, guilt, unhappiness, evil are remediable. But surely the mapping of the mind we still use – id, ego, super-ego and so on – will soon seem like those early charts of the British Isles: colourful guesswork for sure, but crude and misleading.

The appeal of psychoanalysis – I mean the popular appeal, aside from anything therapeutic – is that it reassures you you're not, as you suspect, superficial and transparent. You are *deep*, not what you seem, but an enigma, a labyrinth.

The trouble (for me) is psychoanalysis might stop the Bull bellowing, but not kill it.

flitcraft

Maybe the innermost layer of the Oedipal story is the most obvious – that Oedipus, despite being robbed of his identity at birth, shows he's still Oedipus by fulfilling his terrible destiny. In *The Maltese Falcon* (novel) there's a sub-story that's like a comic or parodic version of the Oedipus myth. Charles Flitcraft, after a brush with death one lunch hour, disappears from his stereotypical suburban life, only to turn up five years later in a different city living a parallel life with, as before, a wife, a kid, a house on a nice street, driving the same model of car.

same-old

Identity has its root in sameness, from *idem* [the same] and *identidem* [the same again and again]. Its original usages in late medieval English were theological (of the same substance) and mathematical (identical equations). I don't suppose there was any reassurance in its metaphoric shift to personhood – more the dispiriting realisation that oneself was the same-old same-old, when really something altogether new would be preferable. Lost, unknown, misplaced, disguised identities are the stuff of folklore, myth, Shakespeare's comedies, and their many contemporary descendants. It's mistaken to think they express fear, or only fear. Our deepest wish is to be not the same person.

Gender is one of the few things about yourself you can change – perhaps the only thing of importance? Not your left-handedness, say, nor eye colour, sense of smell, gait, clumsiness, shyness, not the reflex to gag at the sight of blood.

Derrida got a lot of mileage out of *différance* and its secondary meaning of deferral. Good miles (in my opinion). In English, though, the word has further potential. 'What's the difference?' people say in Ireland, meaning, 'how much do I owe you for that?' Or 'they had a difference' to mean euphemistically there was an irreparable breach, say, between siblings – a sense that's retained generally in the divorce courts, as in 'irreconcilable differences' between the parties. 'Difference' in this context implies disjunctions of balance and perspective that, if not corrected, allow grievances to remain active and fester between people.

Similarity, not difference, is the true opposite of sameness. Sameness is a state where no connection appears – whereas similarity implies both likeness and difference. It gives energy to our yearning to be part of some great whole – and so therefore do simile and especially metaphor, without which we would be dull dogs. Those attributes of language express our longing for connection and thereby belonging – not routinely the state we find ourselves in. This absence of connection is what I think Plotinus meant by 'the

Land of Unlikeness, where, fallen from our resemblance to the Divine, we lie in gloom and mud'.

Admittedly, there are other escapes from, so to speak, the Glastonbury mud. It's just that poems – those few, that is, with the swiftness of metaphor – are what in days gone by I put my shirt on.

The Anglo-Saxons had a nifty trick to think figuratively: they wrote riddles in the first person. And it works! Sylvia Plath's 'Mirror' is a double riddle with the answer as its title.

Those hoary academic terms *tenor* and *vehicle* to 'define' metaphor miss the point. They are useful only to describe conscious forms of figurative thinking like riddles, and also analogies and extended or abbreviated conceits – whereas metaphoric thinking is confused, intoxicated, wriggly, a bucket of eels, alive with unconscious suggestion, as when Macbeth (post murder) says: 'Light thickens, and the crow / Makes wing to th' rooky wood'.

'And yet this great wink of eternity'
    ('Voyages', II)

'my tongue, the buoy / of my brain bobbing in its cloistered sea'
    (*frank: sonnets*)

26

'I washed my steps with butter, and the rock poured me out rivers of oil'

 (Book of Job)

KJV

'People of the clouds, living there like the mist, like the mist sitting resting with arms on knees'

 (Song Cycle of the Moon-Bone)

Wonguri-Mandjigai (Australia)

'Perfume and youth course through me, and I am their wake'

 ('The Sleepers')

Whitman

Tenors can be the hard lads to pin down.

Michael Donaghy wrote a funny poem (a sonnet) with a *literal* tenor and vehicle. The tenor's Pavarotti and the vehicle's a yellow cab. Spoken by an Upper East Side doorman, it finishes (Brooklyn accent): 'Yessir, I put the tenor in the vehicle. / And a mighty tight squeeze it was.'

tenor & vehicle

I was in the toilets of a Dublin pub with Seamus Heaney. As we were drying our hands, an auld lad – a *gurrier* with red face and fawn overcoat – emerged from the only cubicle and went straight out the door. Then he was straight back saying, 'Jaysus, is it yourself?' He held out his hand. 'Put it there!' Seamus took the man's hand and shook it firmly without hesitation. And we left. No comment, and no return to the wash

a handshake

basin either as we resumed our conversation. Out on the street, Seamus donned his felt hat and pulled it low over his forehead. Maybe then just the trace of a smile.

The last time I met SH I recognised him by his gait. Face and upper body were hidden behind a parked lorry, but I saw Seamus was coming along just the same by spotting his legs under the lorry and, for the first time, noticing his nimble feet. I'd a similar experience as I waited outside the Unicorn Theatre in Covent Garden for my adolescent kids to emerge from *The Magic Flute*. A youngish couple came by hand in hand, and the woman looked frankly at me and smiled. I looked away thinking that's a bit cheeky, her giving me the eye like that. Then I glanced after them as they strolled towards Long Acre and saw (too late) my god it was – let's call her Heidi! – an Austrian girl I met as a student in Paris. Her face would have matured, and she was probably wearing make-up. But the rhythm of her stride from behind – which I'd no conscious memory of – triggered recognition.

That ability would have helped in the rainforest to tell at a distance friend from enemy. You can mask a face but not your legs.

I loved Seamus 'this side of idolatry' – as the man said – but I wasn't influenced by his poems. In fact, I felt let down when I first bought *Death of a Naturalist*

at seventeen. I went on to admire, greatly, later books
– and I came to recognise the robustness of that first
book. But its depiction of rural life was for me, living on
a farm at the time, too filtered by its neo-Georgian lens.

One thing in Heaney's work I was drawn to, and it
may have rubbed off, is an unhealthy interest in *corpses*
corpses. Well, maybe not unhealthy, but certainly
culturally specific. I remember seeing as a small
child my mother's first cousin William McGrath – for
the first time that is – laid out on his bed. It was an
elevated bed with a massive mahogany headboard,
much grander than my parents' bed. And everyone *Cousin Willie's*
was remarking how grand Cousin Willie looked, lying
there in his Child of Mary robes and tidily holding his
rosary. He was my first corpse.

Greg Delanty told me his mother was walking home
with her shopping from Cork's English Market. She
was just across the North Gate Bridge when she spot-
ted a neighbour having a smoke outside O'Connor's
Funeral Home. Remembering that her neighbour's *Tommy's*
husband hadn't been well, she enquired how he – let's
call him Tommy – was doing. 'Oh, Tommy's grand,'
the neighbour replied. 'Won't you come inside and
have a look at him?'

Drummond of Hawthornden tells how Ben Jonson
knocked on the chest of Sir So-and-So and asked

him (Sir So-and-So being presumably comatose from drink) if he was within.

Did Nefertiti die of tuberculosis? Yes, says the archaeologist, we have seen the evidence in her bones. Impossible, says the philosopher – Bruno Latour – since the pharaoh's spouse died thousands of years ago, whereas the bacterium that causes TB wasn't discovered until 1882. For sure, the ill-fated queen did not die of TB as the poor of Ireland did in the 1930s and 40s. She may have died – for all we know – of a plague, or a curse, or let's say she succumbed to an evil spirit – just as in medieval times Europeans died of vampirism, and our Romantic ancestors, such as Schiller and Keats, died of phthisis or, more commonly, 'consumption'.

consumption

Three hikers climbed a mountain in the French Alps. The first was a veteran mountaineer on the mend from Covid, who found the climb strenuous but recuperative. The second, his pregnant niece, was at first exhilarated by the air but then, overcome with nausea, had to be carried to the summit by the third, her Senegalese partner who, on his first trip to Europe, was mostly struck by the novelty of snow. Did they climb the same mountain? Maybe there are limits to subjectivity – but it's more fun to think there aren't. The mountaineers did, of course, climb the same mountain; and, of course, they didn't. Ah there's Dr

three hikers

Johnson stubbing his big toe on that damned rock again!

Bishop Berkeley's infamous *esse est percipi* (one exists if observed) came from the study of optics, with his realisation we see an orange in the same way we see a friend is embarrassed, through a cascading sequence of seemingly instantaneous mental inferences. There's no orange on the table (no table either), only that the brain perceives roundness and colour, correlates distance and volume, and instantly computes the logarithm of perspective. Wow, it's an orange – not a kumquat! So, too, your boyfriend reacting – let's say – to that slip you've made about his waistline, is sending out a score of visual cues, and is now glancing at his plate and fidgeting with his knife and fork.

orange

Note: this is commonplace in nature, I mean the instantaneous computation of subtle visual cues. Try swatting a fly! My pond fish recognise me – and only me – when first thing a summer morning I swing wide the courtyard door. They crowd to the surface. They're especially lively when I'm in my orange shorts only, and holding the food jar.

orange shorts

What the fishes' wee brains actually make of my shorts is unclear. Frogs (notoriously adept at catching flies) extract only so-called 'feature detectors' from the visual field. Their eyes are unconcerned with the shape, brightness and colour of things stationary. A frog will starve surrounded by food that doesn't move. The optic fibres respond to edges, curvature, shading, movement – so the composite perceived by the brain may resemble a blob or bead darting here and there against the background. Snap! Food? Not every time. But yum often enough – though not a spectacular visual experience.

snap!

We see through glass because it's a mess, its molecular structure so slovenly that photons have few planes to reflect off or bump into. Light passes through almost unobstructed.

glass, darkly

Beautiful as it is, the verse from 1 Corinthians in the KJV, 'For now we see through a glass, darkly; but then face to face: now I know in part; but then shall I know even as also I am known', is misleading. The image Paul had in his mind was a mirror of polished metal; it's really yourself – not God or truth – you can't yet see clearly.

solid oak

(Arthur) Eddington's infamous table is a fizz of energies in almost empty space. It's not in fact even that, but a teeming concourse of probabilities. Just so (as well) is the 'I' seeing it as solid oak: the brain, the mind, consciousness, spirit – none of which we think of as solid oak.

A very small child, I am sent the short walk out to the farmyard and down the Lane Gate to bring water from the well for tea. As I hold the sweet tin under the icy spout, I hear my mother call my name from the house – and I call back in answer. This became a routine. Fetching spring water was my chore, my 'job'. And my mother would check on me just around the time I was bending to fill the sweet tin. But some mornings there was a delay. She got distracted, I suppose. I would linger with my brimming tin of water in wait for her summons. I'd throw stones in the stream, or poke the frogspawn with a finger, glad no doubt of my chance to do so, but also (I'm thinking) somehow unable to leave the well until I heard my name called. In bed at night as a child, or when I woke in the dark, I was terror-stricken replaying this scenario – which happily didn't last long. Our pump-house was already being built and soon we'd have running water.

Berkeley's '*esse* is *percipi*' (as he wrote) is a perfect expression of the need for belonging. Once separated from the mother – which is in part a desire for adventure – we enter an interim of being on our own, an aloneness in existence that can be salved by friendship, love, parenthood, by weak affiliations such as those to party, country, team, profession, 'followers'. But not erased. Masked, too, by position, fame, self-esteem, feelings of megalomania, invulnerability, perhaps of paranoia. But only masked. Lucky

God

there's an entity – for the bishop, God – keeps the table solid when we've left the room, that kept the moon in motion before we were born, before animal life – before eyesight – evolved, and now upholds the ocean far from human eyes.

2

I was born into a horse-drawn candlelit world. There I am being lifted – it's my first memory outdoors – onto Nance's back at the end of the Long Field where the butt-wheel ruts lead down to the Glens. It must be I've never been this far from our house. The men are all around in open shirts hurrahing, raising bottles of stout, laughing up at me. The little man's first go on a horse!

Now I'm standing in the cot next my mother's bed the night Nance dies. There's shouting and bad language outside as my mother boils pots of scalding water on the open fire and men with storm-lamps race with it in buckets to the far corner of the Big Lawn. Nance is there, whinnying, in trouble foaling. A long moan out of the dark means she is lost. In the morning, I'm taken to see the new foal in the Paddock wobbling on long spindles, while my father is on his knees feeding her milk – as I will a hundred times – from my baby-bottle.

The foal is chestnut, not a grey like her mother. She too is called Nance. I'll hang off her neck. We'll run with me clinging to her mane and ears. I fall off and clamber back up. We plop down together on the headland exhausted. But she grows tall, high-spirited, skittish, and soon speeds away into grown-up life. My father borrows Paton's pony and trap and, with Paton taking the reins, we set out for stud. On the drive back, we stop at the pub in Watergrasshill. It's late when we start again for home under the Great Bear. Paton lashes the pony on, while Nance on a loose tether keeps pace behind. Not long now, my father tells me in a whisper, she'll have a foal of her own.

My mother is sad. Is it because we haven't money, I want to know. But it seems we've enough. It must be she's missing the Old House. She talks about how cool the bedrooms were beneath the thatch in summer, and how she'd station the pram under the rose bower outside the garden door. She complains the rooms here in the bungalow are small and have high ceilings. I love the Old House, too, though I didn't live in it. The thatch has been burned off and it's open to the sky. Beside the hearth in the kitchen there's a wheel-bellows that I turn when a fire is lit to boil oats for the horses. In the hallway is wood panelling you can lift and look behind. That's where someone hides things.

the Old House

Great Aunt Nell, everyone says, returns to the Old House when someone has died. She would have been my father's aunt. I never knew her. My mother tells us how she herself heard the banshee from the Glens the night before Mossy died. That is her brother Mossy, my uncle. I am called after him. His namesake.

Michael The boy holding the birdie in the photo above the mantelpiece is my brother Michael, who died before I was born. My mother talks always about Michael. She says that after he died, months after, my other brother (who's alive) ran in one morning to tell her Michael was coming down the field from the Steps. That she went out to see. I ask my mother who's the boy in the smaller photo holding her hand walking along the busy street. She says it's me – that's us the day we went to Cork. I think my mother has made a mistake. I've never been to Cork.

I'm under the table hiding. There's a man in the room, Tommy Harte. He's painting and talking non-stop to my mother. Tommy is one of the Holy Family. Their cottage is next to the chapel. There's Old Tom the carpenter, Kate his wife, and their son Tommy, who's now hopping up and down off the table as he starts work on the ceiling. Tommy suddenly sticks his head under the table and taps me with his rule on my bottom. Didya think I couldn't see ya! Get out from in under there.

Of the holy pictures and statues around the house, I like best the Infant de Prague in the shrine above the bed. He's a boy with a heavy gold crown and wears a wide cape like Mrs Watt the Master of the Hounds, except his is a brighter purple. In one hand he holds up a ball that has the Cross fixed on top of it. He has a smiling, kind face. But I'm frightened in bed at night by the Sacred Heart and the Holy Ghost.

The gable room of the Old House keeps the geese safe from the fox at night. It's known as Judge's Room. It's where Judge would come to sleep before he was found dead below in Buckley's abandoned dwelling-house. Jim Judge, my father says, walked the length and breadth of Ireland. The Old Garden's no longer in use. The rockery's overgrown with rhododendron, and briars and nettles have sprung up around the apple trees and the mock orange, raspberries, pampas and lilac. On the bare ground under the yew is where my sister's made our cabby-house. It's where I go to her school, where I'm learning Irish and French.

I wasn't born into a horse-drawn candlelit world, of course. It was simply 'the world'. It took on that aspect for me in retrospect – which came about quickly, almost immediately. Lame Jack, the draught horse, and his unbroken mate, Billy, were both put down soon after Nance died and were not replaced – or rather, were replaced by the gunmetal Massey Ferguson tractor that ran on TVO. My father bought it from John Donovan for 500 pounds in the front parlour. Perched on my father's knees I steered it in through our yard gate while everyone stood around cheering.

My first day at Lisgoold School, I'm driven there by my father on the tractor. By now we've electricity and running water, and soon we'll have the Ford Anglia, television, the telephone. Andy Donovan says we're catching up with the rest of Ireland, and Ireland's catching up with the world. Andy Donovan, my mother says, has advanced ideas. I'm given a day off school to go with him, and my father, to the launch of the *Irish Rowan* in Haulbowline dockyard, where Andy works as a master fitter since he came home from England. He explains we're walking across the keel of a future ship, and then the keel of another, and another, before we come into view of the new ship. We watch the wife of the Government Minister let go a bottle that smashes against the prow. The ship starts to slide backwards, slowly at first, then with a loud splash the stern hits the water. She bounces and wobbles unsteadily before finding buoyancy. And then, as the people continue to clap, the ship wheels to starboard and points towards the harbour mouth.

Around about that time Joe arrived. My father came in the house one morning and announced a perfect stranger had walked in the Passage first thing

38

wanting work. My father's at his wits' end. He's no need of labourers nowadays. And this fellow, he can hardly make out a word he says – who is he? Out of jail, a foreign navy or what? And he doesn't know one end of a heifer from the other. But my mother says, you never know, he could be useful. And so, seeing that Judge's Room is taken by the geese, he's installed up in the Loft along with the oats and the mice. It's dry, and after all it's where the men on the run hid winter nights during the war against the Black 'n' Tans.

Joe loves a bit of style. There's a high shine on his boots when he's dressed for the walk to town, and he has on his grey felt fedora and brightly patterned tie. He's off to the pictures. He knows all the Hollywood stars and is on familiar terms with many of the male leads – not in the least overawed by them. Cary Grant and Gary Cooper are not to be mixed up – the one a proper toff, the other a pure cowboy. He says John Wayne couldn't ride a donkey. As for that fraud 'Jimmy' Stewart – he holds him in utter contempt.

Joe comes and goes. My father is back in the house another morning saying he's disappeared, 'gone on furlough'. Later a neighbour will draw attention to a court notice in the *Southern Star* or *The Echo*. 'Joseph O'Sullivan, of no fixed abode, sentenced to three months' hard labour.' Or it could be six months. His crime would be 'vagrancy or breaking and entering' (one of the abandoned houses in the countryside) or once the 'larceny' of clothing from a washing-line. Another time he stole the clothes off a scarecrow. And then one morning, my father is in again to say Joe's back.

When I go to university in Canada, I'll bring Joe back shirts, maybe a couple of the psychedelic ones a girlfriend has mocked. One he particularly favours is patterned with riding crops and jockey caps. He wears it without a tie. By now he's getting old along with my father, who drives him fortnightly to the doctor's in Carrigtwohill. Sheehan, the doctor, has managed to get him a disability allowance, and soon he's given Old Person's accommodation in town. Joe can't believe his luck.

the twins I was thirty before my mother told me about the twins who had died in the Old House. It was when she first married and was not yet herself, as she put it, 'in the family way'. They had taken on a working girl, Ellen, from a smallholding on the Kerry borders. One morning Ellen wasn't bustling about as usual. Thinking maybe the girl was unwell, after some wavering my mother opened the bedroom door and found two babies on the bed wrapped in bloody linen. They were lifeless, though my mother wouldn't of course say for certain they hadn't died in birth. She then saw Ellen herself was already out on the farm. My father was called, and they brought Heskin from the dispensary and got hold of Father O'Connell. What about the Guards? Godsake no! The priest and the doctor managed to hush it up between them. What else could they do? In those days in Ireland, a woman was sure to be hanged.

My mother's telling me this on Holmbush Road in Putney. She's put her legs up to ease the veins, and she's peeling an apple while drinking tea after our day's excursion. It's her first time in London and she's excited. She can't believe how nice people are – how the schoolgirls in those neat braids helped her with the ticket barrier, and even the old gent with the newspaper gave up his seat on the Tube. She was content standing, but she accepted, of course. And then she gets a smile out of the Guardsman at the palace gate. Wouldn't you want to throw something at him, she whispers to me, as he stands impassive beneath the blazing sun in his preposterous rig-out. And then she does a Maggie Thatcher swing of her handbag in his direction. Was that a faint smile under the bearskin? Surely not! Some lad down from the Gorbals, or say Enniskillen, tickled by the accent. But maybe we imagined it.

My mother's telling me this, something she's kept back all these years, not because it's cautionary. Or not consciously. She's having the time of her life, relieved no doubt at this seeming comfort I live in, while being dazzled herself by the spectacle of the streets and the sights, with the crowds going about their daily business, off to work, school, shopping, up and down the escalators, squeezing into trains. And no one's robbing anyone. Somehow – has it brought to the surface herself as a young woman? In her new home, with its orchard and whitewashed stables, its cobbled yard, its bounty of crops and livestock, her whole life before her – then that moment of foreboding, perhaps, when she goes to unlatch Ellen's door.

My mother believes there's some curse on us, on our house, some price we must pay. If my memory is accurate (I'm not sure it is), she will say this six months later when I'm called home one Saturday morning in March for my small nephew's funeral. I can see her demeanour precisely that day. She doesn't look grief-stricken. She is unsmiling, of course, silent – and also looks shrunken, as if drained out in face and body. Yet she's alert, active, nodding to people, shaking hands. I have an uncle (her brother) who finds things to say at length to the stricken parents about the will of God, etc. My mother has his same faith, certainly, but offers no such words.

Ten years on from this, my mother phones me up from home to tell me she's in ecstasy. She's just been back to the specialist and heard she's in the clear. No more of the treatment. She had to tell me the good

42

news immediately, she says, and she repeats she's in ecstasy. Except she says *estasy*. She knows the word but, it seems, has never used it or even sounded it out. It's not a word she's ever applied to herself. But I can tell she means the word correctly. I doubt she's even heard of Bernini but she'll have read Teresa's own words many times over in Catholic Truth Society booklets. And she is now, like Teresa, looking at herself 'from outside herself'. By using this word (one *he'll* know) she's putting herself at my end of the line in applying it to her state of mind. She's being, like the saint was, unassuming and matter-of-fact. She'll be alive another four to five years and she's in ecstasy.

The ICU with the newborns sounds like an aviary, with regular chimes and bleeps, and every so often an ascending alarm-call that's also tuneful. The nurses are Nigerian, Sri Lankan, Irish and Scots, and they keep that rota in their shifts. Tonight it is the Africans. Anna tells me she was taught by Irish nuns. She has scarification on both cheeks and is, I'm guessing, from the Igbo people. She quietly takes us aside to have a word. She wants us to change the name of our son. So we do. *the aviary*

I'm looking out at the HGVs to-and-fro noiselessly on the Hammersmith flyover. Never a let-up, while all night I hold the tiny finger through the porthole in the Perspex crib, watching the mouth open to scream and close without emitting a sound. Every so often I go down the ward to check on Max and Harry – even tinier than ours – sealed in profound untroubled sleep. I like their names, and see they're joined to one of the iconic surnames of the century. Almost certainly, I think, scions of that lucid physician, a refugee in this city – and a steadfast materialist. I quietly give them my blessing, as I have to my own child, for what it might be worth.

The paediatrician brings out the brain scan for me to hold. It resembles a weather-chart of the night sky with broken cloud. He explains it's the grey areas that are dead tissue. That doesn't recover, or very little. I've read books about the brain and can scale up those cloud formations to their neuronal magnitude. I know a newborn's brain – now about the weight of a can of Coke – trebles in size by adulthood. But the bulk of the intricate 'wiring' will happen in the months to come. You mustn't be too optimistic, he says gently. That said, he adds brightly, your son might end up at Oxford, or Cambridge.

The doctor was about my age, Irish, wearing tweeds and brown brogues, even a cable-knit Aran jumper some days. A Plastic Paddy, as a more self-assured generation of Irish immigrants will say. I picture him from some snobby town like Enniscorthy or Fermoy. His mother would be devout, like my mother, but also

44

carry herself up the aisle with an air of social import
ance. The family would have their customary pew,
if not at the front of the church, then in a prominent
position. His father is a leading man of the town, the
chemist perhaps, or the proprietor of a draper shop.
It would have been a relief their son was diligent
enough to get into medicine, but a disappointment
now he's working in a godless London hospital.

When we returned to the hospital a year on for an in-
formal visit, we saw, too, emerging from the lift, the
younger doctor who'd taken it on herself to ignore the
neonatal Apgar score (it was 2). She was pregnant and
didn't acknowledge us. The Irish doctor was surprised
by our visit, having forgotten his request to review the
baby – then he stood wonderstruck at the 'miracle'
we had brought before him. In disbelief, he examined
the little naked body and – in a routine now familiar
to us – manipulated the limbs to check for 'muscle
tone'. And no seizures, you say, fits? None. But can he
see you? Does he respond to your gaze, your voice?
Yes, though not from the other side of a window. He
peers without recognition. Indeed, as if through a
glass darkly.

In the months after my children were born, I had a
fantasy of killing them, to save them before it was too
late from the agony of living. Or rather, I had a fantasy
of the impossibility of it – since I'd have to plan the

death of their mother as well, and those of three far-away grandparents, then onto the several aunts and uncles . . . But by now I was in oblivious sleep. So it was, or soon was, just a harmless insomniac's mantra, supplanting one had served me for years – counting up the pubs and bars I'd been in. That first year, something I'd almost call a 'new self' came to replace the old: this one more deliberately assumed, tougher, not so trustful, quicker to find the mind's construction in the glance or phrase – and one that was, lo and behold, no longer tongue-tied with strangers.

'The love of life, then, is an habitual attachment' – Hazlitt – 'not an abstract principle.'

I was back in Cork and visited Joe several weeks in hospital the summer he died. 'Old comrade', he'd greet me indistinctly. The last time, after supper one fine evening, I drove with my mother. The ward was emptied out. Joe was there in a straitjacket, twisting and convulsing in a cot-bed. His appearance resembled that anatomical caricature where the body is proportioned according to its nerve endings – enlarged hands and feet, narrowed waist, swollen facial features and grotesque lips – except it was pain. There was no God for sure. No one, not even a nurse, to call.

This was some years before in Ireland the morphine cupboard would be unlocked in such cases. My mother had seen suffering like it. I had not. On my own I'd have had the thought to hold a pillow over Joe's face – but would I have had the resolve? If only we could've talked to a doctor, or someone. No one at that hour. We drove home. She called 'Father Dan' – the same priest who'd tried to teach me to swim as a child. Gay to his fingertips he was, but didn't appear to know it, as he kept my rigid body afloat with a soft hand in the small of my back. A self-denying man, I now understand. He offered to say Mass for Joe. But, before my mother would put the phone down, he also promised to go in to see him immediately. When we arrive at the hospital again in the morning, Joe is gone – the ward silent, the metal bed stripped. Praise God, my mother says. The priest must have spoken to someone. It makes me remember that episode from *Sons and Lovers* when the children give a morphine overdose to the dying mother. I think that bit's auto-biographical.

I've climbed into the attic of Ivydale School, or the campanile rather, since it's one of those tiered Victorian edifices with Italianate icing in the manner of Edward Robert Robson. I'm following up a fellow governor's suggestion we auction the school's musical instruments to boost our finances. They've been unused for decades, since the days of the old GLC and a utopian project to give ordinary London kids a musical education. And here, at this remote summit of the building, under dustsheets I find them: a resplendent mute array of strings, woodwind, brass, percussion. I think of that chapter in Mann's *Doctor Faustus* when the narrator contemplates the orchestral instruments in the display cabinets at the house of Adrian's uncle, and conjures from their silence the Faustian magnificence of German music. Generations of South London children (including my own now) have learned their lessons in the rooms below, unaware of this padlocked magical fairground a few flights above their desks.

I see it would take too much organisation – expert help, expense, labour, endless meetings with the council – to transpose the instruments from their enchantment. As I come back to the stairs, the kids are out to play. That shrill amorphous tumult of the schoolyard barely reaches me and, from this height, the faces of the children, including my own, are indistinguishable. But then I do see my son. I recognise his asymmetric gait as he moves gesticulating among the throng alone, no one bothering him. I'm reminded of that cartoon to illustrate the Higgs mechanism that has Margaret Thatcher striding through a roomful of Tory activists, her passage creating a clustering of bodies that moves with her across the floor – except Michael's walk, as indeed Thatcher's would in real life, opens a furrow of space that folds behind him. I think: a better representation of an elementary particle's mysterious passage through the Higgs field would be how his coming into this life gave mass to mine, and continues to give momentum to my days.

3

That Marx despised us peasants seems clear enough from *The Communist Manifesto*. It describes the urban proletariat as 'rescued from the idiocy of rural life' (*dem Idiotismus des Landlebens entrissen*). But the Marxist historian Eric Hobsbawm claims – in mitigation perhaps – that *Idiotismus* retains 'the original meaning of the Greek term *idiotes* from which the current meaning of "idiot" or "idiocy" is derived, namely "a person concerned only with his own private affairs and not with those of the wider community".'

Idios turns up twice in the *Odyssey*. Telemachus tells Nestor, to whom he has come for news of his father, his mission is *idiē ou dēmios* (a personal matter, not public, not 'of the people'); and Menelaus later asks if his quest is *dēmion ē idion* (public or private). The Greeks were mindful of the boundary between the private and the public person. They believed, conventionally I suppose, what's private should stay private. It had no place in the Agora, on the Pnyx or in any public forum – and those who forgot were idiots, presumably. When

loudmouth, horny, roaring drunk Alcibiades crashes
the symposium he's being an *idiot*.

Idios also gives us *idiom*. Aristotle, who had looked
inside the mouth of a frog, used the word to describe
its 'peculiar/distinctive tongue' (*idian glottan*) and the
'peculiar/distinctive noise' (*idian phonēn*) it makes.
We recognise the merit of a distinctive personal id-
iom in a writer and its necessity for the poet – whose
utterance is all the better if it has the force of a blurt
and comes out with vocal fry or some spit: 'We bor-
rowed the loan of Kerr's big ass / To go to Dundalk
with butter' (Patrick Kavanagh).

'Shot the lithe Sleds like Shod vibrations /
Emphasized and gone' (Dickinson)

'The pin-swin or spine-swine / (the edgehog
miscalled hedgehog) with all his edges out'
(Marianne Moore)

'as in the bra ad // the heart lifts and separates,
shrivelled with exultation' (Les Murray)

'My soul within the shades of night / Like a languid
plant with a fungoid blight' (Stevie Smith)

'out of a bush in the darkness, a nightingale's
piercing cries and gurgles' (Lawrence)

It's better to sound like a frog than a nightingale, if you're a frog; it's probably better to be counted one of the frogs, if you're a poet.

It would be some upset for the books were the first great narrative sweep of the *Odyssey*, a young man's quest for his father (the so-called *Tēlemacheia*), a personal matter only, not of public concern. Of course, it's both. That's the paradox often of poems: their material is fear, loss, illicit love, secret guilt – private stuff pushed out, freed or, even better, making its own bolt into the arena of public spectacle. It helps when you're an *eejit*.

The *Symposium* was turning into a rather long-winded dispassionate account of Eros until Alcibiades showed up dressed as Dionysus.

I remember the unimpeded eloquence of childhood. I'm standing on a chair outside our front door to deliver a jeremiad upon those within and doing it with a conviction of lucidity and fearless righteousness. I learn only from the alarm of my sister, and then my mother, my speech is unintelligible except for a few words they find shockingly obscene. And then it was gone, incapacitated by some obscure injury, or, as I suspect, a congenital tendency reinforced by embarrassment: *Has the little boy lost his tongue!*

The most private part of the self – its pudendum, so to speak, its place of shame – is located at the back of the tongue, where speech is formed, or malformed, or struggles to be formed, at a threshold or crossing-place between the darkness of the material body and the cave-mouth to light – beyond which lie in prospect the playing fields of the soul.

It's wrong to assume writing has to do with fluency. It's often more to do with a lack of it. It helps to have an impediment, a stammer or to have been literally tongue-tied as a child. I nattered away to my mother but clung to her when there was company. For thirty-plus years, it was impossible to initiate conversation with strangers, to talk on the phone or speak up in groups. I reckon this may have given me a head start as a poet.

'A hesitation' – Zofia Kalińska – 'is not the same as a pause. It is an attempt to defeat the wish.'

'A heavy ox stands on (my) tongue' (*bous epi glōssē megas / bebēken*) – spoken by the Watchman at the outset of the *Oresteia*. Even as the words are uttered, the ox moves its hoof and the tongue is freed for speech. The Greek imagination pivots from the adolescent sulks and manlike slaughter at Troy to retribution in the House of Atreus. Onstage, or rather just 'offstage' in the Greek theatre, are infanticide, incest, the blinding, the bedroom murder; onstage, these events

52

are recounted, exposed, mediated; or rather they are replayed before an audience who know the story and see emerge from the void the masked actors, who with measured words give voice to the unspeakable.

The Greeks discovered drama, or stumbled on it, when Aeschylus (as the old Loeb edition put it) 'brought in the second actor'. With that, everything from the *Agamemnon* to *Phèdre* to *Krapp's Last Tape* and *Breaking Bad* became a matter of time. Borges: 'Along with the second actor came dialogue and the indefinite possibilities of the reaction of some characters upon others. A prophetic spectator would have seen that multitudes of future apparitions accompanied the second actor: Hamlet and Faust and Sigism[o]ndo and Macbeth and Peer Gynt, and others whom our eyes cannot yet discern.'

St Paul said the Crucifixion was *skandalon* (σκάνδαλον) to the Jews, literally a stumbling-block, figuratively a scandal; whereas to the Gentiles it was *moron*, mere stupidity, moronic – not real. As Borges observed of Tacitus, the greatest historian of the Roman world, he failed to perceive the Crucifixion, though he recorded the execution of Christ.

1 Corinthians 1:23

stumbling-block

A writer – any artist or thinker – should want to cause scandal in the Pauline sense: be brazen about whatever affronts the conformist and bourgeois mind.

ingress

Ideally, a reader gasps, the audience hisses, in discomfort. This, not for notoriety, not just to take the lobster on a stroll around the block, but to punch a hole in the plasterwork of one's own habitual thinking and allow ingress to what's unconscious, irrational, forbidden – to allow some unsavoury leakage into the sentence.

Leviticus 19:14

Paul was remembering *skandalon* from Leviticus in the Greek Septuagint. There the original Hebrew means a trap or tripwire, any device that causes a person to stumble, slip, fall; to sin, lose faith; to transgress.

leg-over

In a poem, the device of enjambement, of literally 'throwing the leg over', has the effect of acceleration, of hurrying the reader on with the excitement of discovery – with, I'd suggest, the transgressive thrill of stumbling on illicit things. As Milton tells us in his preamble to *Paradise Lost*, 'the sense [is] variously drawn out from one Verse into another'; and it has for him a political aim: that 'of ancient liberty recover'd'.

swift horses

Leopardi: 'The beauty and delight of . . . vigorous, swift styles . . . derive chiefly from this, that [they] keep the mind in constant and lively movement and action, transporting it suddenly, and often abruptly, from one thought, image, idea, or object to another, and often to one very remote and different: so the mind must work hard to catch hold of them all, and, as it is flung hither and thither, it feels invigorated, as one does in walking quickly or when being carried along by swift horses.'

Yeats's 'Leda and the Swan' caused scandal when it was published. Such an abstruse, esoteric poem? But the girl's 'nape', the 'white rush', those cl/amorous wings, the predatory beak that turns 'indifferent' after the act – it's hard to miss the pressure of the wish, its energy felt in the swift-running syntax of the verse. Not so surprising, then. Though I don't suppose anyone – even Willie himself? – tripped on the word 'bill', first used for the beak.

Wild Swan

Did Yeats wear his white suit when he proposed marriage to Iseult Gonne? As he writes in old age, among school children, 'I had pretty plumage once.'

'Underneath all reason lies delirium, and drift' – thus spake Deleuze and Guattari.

'Man will become immeasurably stronger, wiser and subtler' – Trotsky – 'his body will become more harmonised, his movements more rhythmic, his voice more musical.' And people did – so far as physical attributes went – on the Soviet murals.

Literature and Revolution

For millennia the copy was the key artefact of civilisation, the copyist its keeper. Each copy was itself a unique product, painstakingly made by a single hand,

the copy

and mind, and necessarily imperfect. Its validity was underpinned by the belief we ourselves were copies of the Divine – every one of us imperfect, identifiable in our imperfections, but each also a true reflection of the original.

The printed book became the prototype of capitalist production, its success replicated in a plenitude of commodities and brands, from Bird's Custard to cigarette packets, soap powders, soup cans, Boeing 747s. The brand supplanted the Divine. It guaranteed sameness and underwrote value. Even so, market value can be transformed by ownership and use, as we learned from Warhol, whose silkscreen *Mona Lisa*s just about compete in price with the original – and whose washcloths, had he thought to sign them, would be as coveted as Madonna's cone bra and Maradona's shirt.

Into the history of replication comes the body, every intricate material segment of which is re-growable, for sure, by means of slick genetic choreography. Clones, we say – presuming a clone would be *other*. But one psychological effect of getting old is to doubt one has a unitary self that can last that long. I have photographic recall, for example, of my first girlfriend, Marie Smart, falling over at Midleton Horse Show and me running to kiss her. The sole keeper now of this (precious!) memory is, well, *my memory*, a faculty often with graphic and, I like to think, accurate recall – but it's

56

also a promiscuous inventor of dreams and fictions as well as owning vast featureless expanses, months and even years, with entire torrid episodes wiped, only for one, on occasion, to be unaccountably recovered. What happens if tearful toddling Marie, along with a few thousand similarly poignant memories, were transferred as a 'bundle' to the new brain? Hmm.

It seems likely the entity methinks is 'I' could be usurped and seamlessly replicated. Out goes old *cogito*, and its counterpart for Spinoza and Kant. Or: has someone died during the procedure? The perfect murder.

Freud loved murder mysteries. Figures.

Two of my political heroes were, indeed are, Tony Benn and Yasser Arafat, the former for his renunciation of aristocratic privilege, and the latter because (whatever his deep and consequential faults) he embodied the pride of a defeated people – a pride that was manifested in the two young cadets at his tomb in Ramallah, boys really, who, having ascertained I was Irish (*Irish-Irish!*), presented arms in my honour.

I met Benn late on in his life, at some literary do in the West Country, where I failed to get him started in conversation about Arafat, I think because he was having difficulty reading my lips. Instead, it was easier to listen to his story of flying over Europe in wartime,

57

a stunning tale of derring-do about clumsily dropping into enemy territory a hapless agent who then, against the odds, survived. I understood it was an experience he'd had as a pilot in the Second World War. But when I looked it up years later, it turned out to be about his father – also a pilot – in the First World War.

Aymara

I did manage (I think) to communicate my obsession at the time with Aymara – a language with trivalent logic: that is, it allows something to be true or false, or also both, and neither. We were in a long room with French windows open at either end, and I tried to clarify this by pointing to the fact it was, just then, raining if you looked out one window, while it was dry looking out the other: *it was raining/it was not raining/it was both, and neither.* He was attentive but seemed nonplussed, and kept looking back and forth between my lips and the far ends of the room.

backwards to the future

Aymara is one of few languages that posits the future as behind us, while the past lies ahead. So one moves – or is moved – backwards into a marriage, parenthood, a strange city, any new situation, and as time passes we see coming into view in front of us, and then clear as day, how it all turned out. The future's hidden, the past in plain sight. Makes sense.

The reason we resist letting the future overtake us from behind is it removes the limited degree of volition we feel we have before us: I'm going to knock on this door, I will ask that stranger on a date, I'm going to put my shirt on that horse. The outcome is unknown; fair enough, I'll try my luck. What we find harder is not knowing something that's already been decided. Any writer who's been shortlisted for a prize has experienced how uncomfortable it is to sit there at the so-called Awards Ceremony knowing the decision's made, the name already in the envelope, and some bastards in the room are apprised of what it is. We're players in a cruel charade on behalf of some flash PR outfit or to gratify a boor with millions.

Of course, if the name turns out to be one's own, all is forgiven.

Of course, if the name turns out to be someone else's, enemies are made.

There is a curious aftermath here – let's call it Post-Prize Stress Disorder. The brain has engaged, even though one sternly resisted, with the scenario of success. The postures of acceptance have been imagined, the gracious phrases rehearsed, the feigned humility, the gratuitous gratitude and so on. This imagined outcome doesn't just instantly shrivel up or self-destruct. It'll take a week or two. Alas, when we experience big losses, the great sadnesses, the psychology is the same – and the shadow outcome continues its existence, dream-heavy and wish-borne, and will maintain its trajectory for, well . . . who knows how long.

A run of hard luck crushes only those whom life has favoured, since they never imagined misfortune could overtake them. I read that somewhere.

The mythic appeal of Schrödinger's Cat is it offers an indefinite reprieve from certainty.

The Book

The notion our lives are fatal, pre-destined, already written down in The Book (if not inside the mythic box or envelope) is ancient and persistent. We simply turn the pages. But we cannot skip ahead – there can be no spoilers, it turns out, despite the claims of oracles and fortune-tellers. Fatalism accords with fundamental physical law, which observes no past or future and cannot account for our unfolding experience of time, nor the contingencies we associate with chance and with free will. But fatalism accords, I believe, with certain of my own experiences when, under the stress of a life-changing event, the light brightens intensely, the page is suddenly clear, the import of the remainder of my pages dimly foreshadowed.

When my kids were born – twins – I was given one to hold with the information he was dead. After some time, the newborn baby showed signs of life. The young paediatrician said something like *oh no, I hope that's not going to happen again* and she took him away. Again, after some time – perhaps a lot of time (in this context the passing of time becomes chaotic) – she returned in tears to say he was breathing independently. And so it has continued.

The fate of most newborns is to be prey. Those who survive learn to prey. Different for the most part if you're a mammal – and certainly so if you're a human one, though not without exception. Foals and lambs bond tenderly with their mothers, and separation causes distress – you've only to listen to sheep re-establishing kinship ties at shearing time. It would break your heart. Only humans, of course, turn abandoning their young, or killing and eating them, into the Oedipal myth, the Medea story, the feast of Thyestes.

infanticide

Isn't it odd to have cannibalism, even as a symbolic act, at the core of a major religion – or maybe it's not? Maybe to believe without doubt in the deity, we need proof that we share – or have some part of – their supernatural being by eating 'them'. It's not about belief in the Doubting Thomas sense. Rather, we need to know the god's vulnerability is the same as ours, and so we have to be certain – vicariously, for sure – we really have killed them.

Doubting Thomas

Maybe that's what Thomas was after?

It enhances belief in Jesus when you think he himself didn't know. He rode on the donkey into Jerusalem aware the hour had come, since it accorded with Scripture, but not knowing what the hour would bring. As the crowds with palm fronds surged in triumph around him, he didn't foresee that the few days ahead to Passover would mean betrayal, humiliation and the utter defeat of his movement. On the Cross, Jesus proclaims the psalmist's words in Aramaic: *Eli, Eli, lama sabachthani?* ('My God, my God, why hast thou forsaken me?'). It's not crucifixion that confounds him but that his God could abandon him.

The real meaning of this (I think) is Jesus accepts the Father does not exist, or no longer exists as a personal god. Not a loving parent.

The 'Resurrection' confused things.

Suffering is now: that's the image of the Passion. We're enjoying our lives – making music, money, friends, mischief, cocktails, love – while our neighbour endures unbearable suffering. Fair enough, it's not our turn. But Jesus stays on the Cross throughout, as in every bedroom of my childhood, eternally hanging as a sign above those whose faith it is that the power who put all in motion and who, witnessing the – possibly unforeseen – tragedy of our foolishness and vulnerability, took pity, saying *I'll suffer this living and dying so you can do likewise.* Thus we, too, can become godlike.

I'm an altar boy in my spotless starched surplice. A perk of the job is to sit sidewise on the altar steps facing the congregation and watch the girls in my class come up for Communion. Helen, Ann, Mary, Anna-Mary, Kathleen, Assumpta, Veronica, Catherine – all eight colourful in their Sunday frocks, newly confessed, in single file, demure, vestal. Out the corner of my eye I can see the crucifix that's somehow wangled its way into Lisgoold chapel. Caravaggio-esque. The loincloth isn't knotted – not so I can tell – and one imagines it's about to slip off or blow away. The flesh is freshly painted, the Nureyev-like alabaster legs are crossed, with the right foot lightly resting on the left and nailed to it with a dollop of blood. *Caravaggio in Lisgoold*

If there were a redemptive being or force, it would need to redeem us first from the nightmare of exponential replication – or rather, the nightmare it is to us, creatures who evolved for local survival, capable of devotion to immediate kin, and just about capable of extending goodwill to a community the size of a fishing village. All else requires the delirium of the crowd. *delirium*

Mass culture occupies the greater part of our day-to-day experience. Think sports, soaps, *Star Trek*, *E.T.*, *Gandhi*; think Beanie Babies, Rubik's cube, the

Swoosh; a papal conclave, Kumbh Mela, the People's Princess. It's disrupted, of course, by sickness, break-ups, money troubles, misfortune's countless faces, by occasionally, er, reading a good book.

Playground bullies, rioters, the Roman mob, concert-goers, Twitter pile-ons: humans want to run in herds. Who hasn't got carried away at a football game, or even watching the match on TV? It's the tribal war-whoop for sure – the whole village chasing the bison, the overwhelming urge to slaughter the next village that, upon defeat, is readily redirected at a scapegoat. But there's something existential that underpins it. Who does not feel in the concert hall or at the late-night karaoke that blissful respite from the anvil-hammer of the self?

We are born, like Miranda, into a paradise 'that has such people in it', an island-world of easy access for the wide-eyed ego. It's an adjustment to move to the class-room – one not easily made, hence the regularity of school shootings. But once the self is absorbed into the class, we are ready for the choir, the team, the Scouts, the gang, the solidarity of a brick-throwing mob and – thrillingly – the screaming, packed stadium.

As the roars resound around the ground, which one was me?

Contingency is a new concept with regard to human destiny – well, new-ish, a departure of the Enlightenment but one often resisted, by Spinoza and notably by Newton, who viewed his discoveries as recoveries. Likewise, writers have good reason to favour the idea it's all been around before. Nothing can add to Sophocles, Lucretius, Ovid et al. All we can hope to do is 'make it new' in the sense of renovation only, to give it our distinctive idiom – that *it* being a given. Poetry is always a work of translation. Arguably.

'Plagiarism is necessary,' according to the Comte de Lautréamont. 'It clasps the author's sentence tight, uses his expressions, eliminates a false idea, replaces it with the right idea.' As I think I must have read elsewhere: 'The history of literature – a secret history no one can write except in part, because authors are skilful at obscuring themselves – is a sinuous garland of plagiarism.'

a sinuous garland

'Isn't it amazing how she evokes soul, body, hearing, tongue, sight, skin, as though they were external and belonged to someone else? And how at the same moment she both freezes and burns, is irrational and sane, is terrified and nearly dead, so that we observe in her not a single emotion but a whole concourse of emotions?' This could be from any gushy, if rather well written, contemporary poetry review or 'blurb'. But it is Longinus writing in the first century about

φαίνεταί μοι

Sappho's Fragment 31 (which he's just saved, though he doesn't know it, from oblivion).

It seems not to occur to Longinus that Sappho was writing a poem. It's the greatest possible tribute – but it is a fallacy. Whatever Sappho's own experience of love, she was not freezing and burning while she composed. She may have been in a sweat, shaking, in suspense or have become overexcited about how nicely it was coming along. She might well have been thinking *wait till that gobshite Alcaeus* – her arch-rival – *gets wind of this!*

There's zero connection between the intensity of a poet's feelings and the intensity their words transmit. If there were, we wouldn't need poetry, or any other art. 'In the bad type of the thin pamphlets' – Randall Jarrell – 'people's hard lives and hopeless ambitions have expressed themselves more directly and heartbreakingly than they have ever been expressed in any work of art'.

cold hearts   'Lyric poets usually have' – Miłosz – 'cold hearts.' Or better: hearts that are just turning cold.

the sublime   Longinus was writing of 'the sublime'. Not a defined term – rather, a category to include turbulent forces, violent energies, awesome spectacles of nature and human passion that is matched in expression by a vehement and figurative style. It fits well with the 'enthusiasm' of James Thomson's *The Seasons* (1730). But the daimonic power of the Romantic imagination a half-century or so later is outside its scope – in those vertiginous flights of transcendence that have rightly become our touchstones for the sublime.

Where might we look for our own sublime in the past half-century? It's here and there . . . in Ashbery, Ted Hughes, *passim* in Les Murray, Neruda if we cast further. It seems to arise from our feeling of distance – but not our banishment – from the Spirit. Larkin's 'High Windows', which starts out in the locker-room and ends with Shelley's 'white radiance of Eternity', is a telling instance. Infrequent though such moments are, I'd bet my last molar they are all that will survive of us after the Second Great Dying.

If just a few fragments survive, let this be one:

Life and the memory of it cramped,
dim, on a piece of Bristol board,
dim, but how live, how touching in detail
– the little that we get for free,
the little of our earthly trust. Not much.
About the size of our abidance
along with theirs: the munching cows,
the iris, crisp and shivering, the water
still standing from spring freshets,
the yet-to-be-dismantled elms, the geese.

Late on in life, I spent a winter in Paris. A northern city. Cold, grey as London. I'd stay in my room drinking awful coffee and work till noon, then head for the Marché Monge or walk down rue Mouffetard to buy wine and charcuterie. After lunch I went to a cinema or I ran in the Luxembourg Gardens – the Orangerie sealed, the boat pond half frozen over, the Carrousel in chains. Then, an afternoon in February, the concrete sky gave way to aquamarine. On my jog, the park benches were occupied by frail men in woolly scarves and women, not all of them elderly, in boots and furs, their heads thrown back and angled towards the solar disc flaring above Montparnasse. A few days later, the grey slab back in place, I cycled to the Marmottan and stepped into its world of light: foliage, fruits, harvest, ripening flesh, dazzling waterscapes, yachts, dancers, acrobats. Paint. Paris is northern but its soul is stained with the south.

paint

Some months before his death, Proust emerged from his apartment and went to the Jeu de Paume to see Vermeer's *View of Delft* – his mission, to find a 'little patch of yellow' he'd read about in the newspaper. He located it on the painting, and it revived him enough to go see the Ingres next door, then lunch at the Ritz. This escapade left him so 'shaken and alarmed' he never left his sickroom again. But he fared better than Bergotte, the fictional vehicle for the episode in *La Prisonnière*, who dies of a stroke before the Vermeer:

68

'In a celestial pair of scales there appeared to him, weighing down one pan, his own life, while the other contained the little patch of wall [*le petit pan de mur*] so beautifully painted in yellow.'

the scales – encore!

Yellow is the loudest colour, and the most contrary. The colour of 'my true love's hair' is also the mark of cowardice; the aura of the risen Christ, the Divine colour, is the tint of a jaundiced baby; the Jewish badge of Nazi Europe, the colour favoured by Klimt's Viennese femmes fatales. It's *The Yellow Book*, Big Bird, the saffron robe, the hue of Homer Simpson's skin, the colour both of gold and of shit. Goethe: 'By a scarcely perceptible change, the beautiful impression of fire and gold is transformed into one not undeserving the epithet foul; and the colour of honour and joy reversed to that of ignominy and aversion.'

yellows

The cone receptors in the retina are not, I read, receptive to yellow. Our eyes normally pick out from the spectrum the wavelengths of just three colours: blue, green and red. The colour the brain actually sees depends on the relative intensity of the wavelengths (which cause brightness or 'luminance'). We see red, as one would expect, when red wavelengths predominate, green when green ones are in ascendancy. When blue's short waves overwhelm the indolent bands of green and red, we see blue. But when the green and red cones are *both* excited to near peak intensity, it's then – strangely – we see yellow. Apart from, say, looking at snow (when all three sets of cones are firing at full blast) it's the most excitation the eye receptors get.

Yellow was the last colour Borges could make out before blindness.

There's no yellow in Rimbaud's 'Voyelles': 'A noir, E blanc, I rouge, U vert, O bleu'. Or is there? 'O, suprême Clairon plein des strideurs étranges' (O, great trumpet full of strange stridencies). Lévi-Strauss argues that yellow discloses its presence 'après le bleu . . . par l'étymologie évidente du mot <<clairon>> . . . et par la couleur de cet instrument'. So: we see *through* the blue to the yellow of the O.

It's acceptable to wear yellow under a blue coat, but *gaudy* to have blue under a yellow coat, according to Kant.

Would Proust have gotten out of bed for blue? Not from his deathbed.

I wonder if Lévi-Strauss was *hearing* some intimation of Miles Davis in those *strideurs étranges*? The mellowness of jazz trumpet played with a mute: at once intimate and distant, near and far-off, like the lovely effect of wood pigeons cooing.

Blue? Residue of Zyklon B, as well as a consequence of Rayleigh scattering. Goethe says its effect is 'well-nigh indescribable'. Del. *well-nigh*! We live on the blue planet, and that gives us a cool privileged nice sort of feeling. The sky, the ocean, the distant mountains are pleasing to the eye. But imagine blue as our immediate colour, the colour of leaves and of grass? It would drive us mad.

Last time I was in South Kensington I walked by 69 Cromwell Road. Still no blue plaque. It's where Yves Klein lodged when he had an apprenticeship nearby in a restorer's workshop, where he learned about the raw materials of paint and took home cardboard off-cuts – those, he painted blue.

When going blind, Derek Jarman made *Blue*, the movie, with its single continuous frame of Klein Blue. Blue is the realm for sure of the solitary spirit, of Satan's long fall into Hell, the doomed astronaut's slow drift from the mother ship, the soul's last journey from the body (as I imagine it).

'The Blue Danube', 'Blue Velvet', 'Blue Train', 'Blue Suede Shoes', 'Lady Sings the Blues', 'Rhapsody in Blue'. No one can doubt blue is *moody*. (But Marge Simpson's hair is something else.)

We all know someone who thinks our new blue linen jacket is green and can't be dissuaded. It's infuriating! But it's testimony that sensory experience is subjective – or rather, it's partly subjective (even Wittgenstein would concede, I think, the jacket is *some* colour).

Kant

As with colour, so with all that comes through the senses? All that can come to us. The glass is thick, and dense with subjectivity. I don't doubt we impose categories on our experience, that most of it is a function of habit, psychology, language. But I've lived too long, too precariously, not to give *some* credence to what happens – and not to hope there's some glorious recompense in 'other' worship', whether of the beloved, the divine form, the mountain, the aria, the child, the pet. Or the lot of them! I guess I'd settle in the end for some Kantian in-between. But don't quote me.

'[W]ho has not mastered the Kantian philosophy' – Schopenhauer – 'remains stuck in the grasp of that natural and childish realism in which we are born'. Oh well, too late now, maybe.

mysteries

We live *inside* the mysteries, for sure. Two I've a sense of: one being time, and the other of course language, through which we have created the religions, the political systems, our science, ourselves. Language didn't antedate us; it's not some transcendent

72

given, though it may seem like that. It is historical, and therefore, like our political inheritance, should be subject to steady and perhaps radical change. But this it isn't: language is the labyrinth we're enmeshed in, and any line of exploration we think is leading us out only adds a further strand to the entanglement.

'That sweet juice' – Carlo Rovelli – 'that contains all the ambrosia and all the gall of life.' Time. We experience it through its effects: we know we're ageing from the aches and hair loss; our understanding of it is a vast extrapolation, an elaborate network of inferences we accept without question. For we have no direct sensory experience of time (Aristotle). And the psychological means we develop to process it are inefficient and wayward. My children are thirty-five this October – *nel mezzo del cammin* – but before my brain can make that numeric and literary calculation, I'm seeing them only as young adults. When I dream of children, my own and others, their ages are either indeterminate or slide around a scale between infancy and, roughly, pre-teen. Like everyone, I'm familiar with the long dead who turn up alive in my dreams, while the living are always younger, and myself always much younger. We bash our brains to counteract the inability to process time. The tools we use are memory and anticipation. The latter is volitional and is the more effective. Ten minutes to catch that train, one book before I'm thirty, a baby or two under pressure from the, er, 'biological clock', and so on; mortgages, work schedules, pension pots, the lifespans of pets and appliances – they all help. We follow a penal regime, attended by hope and anxiety, and at odds with our diurnal and seasonal rhythms, which are so pleasingly repetitious.

The sweet recurrences of festival and season are not circular but 'spiralar', elongating rings that alas – unlike spirals – allow no spring-back, or none we know of. Memory began from evolutionary pressure: from the urgency to locate the whereabouts of last year's waterhole; the need to recognise the patterns of the returning seasons by spotting cues from clouds and wind changes; as well as from the daily imperative of telling kin from enemy. Hominids acquired powers of recall that were honed generation by generation until they were swift and involuntary – mental reflexes that now often return us unprompted to grief or remorse. But memory, I can attest, grows more selective as we get older, becomes unexpectedly elastic and is – if we're to credit Montaigne – our one consolation.

Montaigne had an untrustworthy memory, though. Or so he tells us.

Adolescence is one phase in life – pregnancy, I imagine, would be similar – when our experience of time feels apparent, when physical body changes, both those that are graduated and sudden, roughly match our calendar experience. I guess the depredations of old age will be the same.

'Age is the bilge we cannot shake from the mop' – Robert Lowell, the year of his death.

bilge

As a young man I was polite with my elders (and I was kind to them when the need arose) but they were to me as sheep grazing on a hillside. Not relevant. Now when I'm enjoying myself among youngsters, and I like to, I cannot long suppress a surge of envy they will still be talking, flirting, joking, drinking in the hours and days after I die.

The 'me' I'm looking at in the mirror, it's not me. It looks and is alien. Yes, there is a me I recognise – a creature not unlike a house dog, often resting comfortably while I read or type or talk with friends on the home phone, or somewhat more active while I garden, cook, or when I teach. This me is by and large a contented and accommodating beast, though capable of being vicious and vociferous in argument, but usually only when the argument is silent and internal.

me

I was back at the eye clinic, this time with my ophthalmologist – a gentle Prod from the Glens of Antrim who is devoted to the poetry of Seamus Heaney. He tells me the happiest thing in the world for him – i.e. 'the finest music' – is to look into the eyes of a small child, so immaculate is the retina. Then adds, it doesn't last long. But he has discharged me. Nothing much wrong with your eyesight, he says, for now.

Though I fear blindness, I believe it could have been a more profound experience of the world than the one I've had. If there were Heaven, I imagine death would be like going from darkness into a room of Renoir and Matisse, where the profusion of colour would 'resolve' as the music of Bach – or perhaps the singing of Callas.

There's Argos, Bran and Sceólang, there's Bill Sikes's terrier Bullseye, Belinda's lapdog Shock, Lawrence's mongrel bitch Bibbles . . . But I can think of no more fictional dogs, and few other pets, that are not allegories or caricatures – and none in poetry. Yet flesh-and-blood pets, dogs especially, haunt the densest thickets of our affections. Every childhood has the pup who snuggled under the duvet, jumped in the car to go to the seaside, posed next to the Christmas tree; who went from bounding over dunes and snowdrifts to dozing ever closer to the fire; who was put down one drear November while we were away at school or in our first job. And then there's the dog, or perhaps cat, we were persuaded to get after life settled and who, in turn, is there among the balloons and wine bottles till the break-up, the bankruptcy or till the kids

are flown. And last, there's the one who might see us
out – another stray, perhaps, or an unwanted bequest
(like the Great Dane in Sigrid Nunez's novel) – who'll
decline as we decline and whose end will bring the
sharpest pang, unless it lives on to pine for us.

The Friend

I forgot about Crab, the mutt in *The Two Gentlemen
of Verona* who, among other heinous crimes, pisses
under the Duke's table. And, of course, we can't for-
get Lear arraigning his 'dog-hearted daughters' in the
guise of the hounds 'Tray, Blanch, and Sweetheart'.
It's unjust to dogs, and by implication to Cordelia –
though it is her 'Nothing, my lord' first unleashed his
rage, that pert daughterly impertinence puncturing
the puffed-out patriarchal ego. Hazlitt: 'the indiscreet
simplicity of her love (which, to be sure, has a little of
her father's obstinacy in it)'.

oops!

I suspect Shakespeare didn't often make it home to
Stratford and hadn't observed his daughters growing
up. I've a hunch he caught up again with his first
daughter Susanna when she was a young woman,
following the death of Edmund, his brother the actor,
who was buried in Southwark by the river. She is
Marina, Perdita, Miranda.

*Shakespeare's
lost heroine*

And Imogen? 'An only daughter is the heart's nee-
dle' is said by Sweeney in the late medieval tale *Buile
Suibne* (Sweeney's Madness), when he is told, falsely,

that his little girl is dead. *Snaithad chroidhe dano ein ingen* in the original – *ingen* being Middle Irish for daughter, from which the name Imogen, or properly Innogen, comes. But I suppose Shakespeare couldn't have known that?

skiving

On the top margin of a manuscript of Cassiodorus' Latin Commentary on the Psalms, preserved in the library of Notre-Dame at Laon, are these words, *isém linn indiu bloscad innagréne frisinnamargánu leth-rati*, written there around 800 by an Irish scribe (on the skive, I fear, from scribing). They lay unread – then unreadable, their language unknown – until construed and transcribed by the German scholar of Old Irish Kuno Meyer around 1910.

isém linn indiu

Such a lovely day
I pause to let the sun's rays
illumine the page

More than 1,000 years the verse waited. A tree was falling in a forest; an arrow stayed in mid-flight; the cat slept on inside the sealed box.

'Not in time but with time' – Augustine – 'God created the world.'

ACKNOWLEDGEMENTS

I am grateful to the Bogliasco Foundation for a Fellowship in 2023 that gave me the opportunity to complete *Rope*.

The lines on p. 67 from 'Poem' by Elizabeth Bishop (Copyright © The Alice H. Methfessel Trust, 2011) are reprinted from *Poems* by permission of Farrar, Straus and Giroux (US) and the Random House Group (UK). The phrase 'a sinuous garland of plagiarism', p. 65, is taken from Roberto Calasso, *La Folie Baudelaire* (Allen Lane – Penguin Books, 2012). In addition, I owe unforgivable debts to the numerous writers – ancient and modern – who unwittingly contributed material to *Rope* (I can only apologise for my wayward recollection, at times, when using it).

I am deeply indebted to Faber's editorial team for their expertise, specifically to: Jane Feaver for her early recommendations and encouragement; Lavinia Singer for her invaluable suggestions and oversight of the editing process; Kate Hopkins for her scrupulous interrogation of the text when copy-editing the manuscript; Kate Ward for her resourcefulness in designing the book. I am especially thankful to Faber's Poetry Editor, Lavinia Greenlaw, for her belief in the work.

I am grateful to Jon Turney and James Gardner for feedback, and for drawing attention to errors and aberrations that, in most instances, I have tried to rectify. My thanks to Michael, Niamh and Susan for reading the manuscript and reviewing some of the more personal material. My warmest gratitude is to Kathryn for her role in the genesis of the book and for her devoted support at every stage of writing.

An extract from *Rope* appeared in *The Great River Review* 72 (Spring 2025).